Daily Alignment Journal

Sephyrus Press
Copyright © 2020 Rachel Archelaus
Intuitive Art Academy, LLC
All Rights Reserved.

You can learn more about Intuitive Art
and Rachel Archelaus at intuitiveart.com

My sincerest thanks to Esther, Jerry, and Abraham for creating such a vivid language with which to discuss alignment, attraction, and who we really are.

INTRODUCTION

No matter what specifics we want to appear in our life—a new love, a fabulous car, a road trip with friends—the truth is that we want those things because we desire the feeling they will produce.

The good news is that feeling great is always within reach if we do some preparation. By focusing in a certain way, we can add velocity to our emotions and build a solid momentum of feeling better and better.

This accomplishes our first goal (feeling good) but also makes it so that we are primed to receive the physical manifestation. We put ourselves in the best position to have our life's dreams play out in front of us. But, most importantly, we practice knowing that we are the creator of our lives.

By focusing deliberately on feeling good and appreciating what we have, we get to notice how that changes our life. As we build trust in this vibrational cause and effect, we free ourselves of all of the "shoulds" and limiting statements we've heard about what we have to do to achieve success.

We learn through our own experience that how we feel is a direct cause to how our lives play out. It's that simple. And you have complete control over it. Woohoo!

This journal is designed to help you focus on what you love and appreciate about your life while at the same time diminishing resistance. The prompts are largely based on the words and work of Abraham-Hicks because they are a shining example of the power of vibration. Not to worry if you aren't familiar with them or their vernacular; I'll describe each section of the journal here so you know how to best use its design.

This journal is a focusing tool for feeling better and developing the habit of checking in with how you feel. Each day starts with the prompt:

How do I want to feel today?

This is your place to feel into your body for what would be ultimately pleasing to you. It can change from day to day or stay the same for weeks. Feel around for an emotional word like: excited, calm, centered, abundant, etc. You can choose one feeling or many, there is no way to get this wrong. The only thing I would watch for is that if you try to use your mind you might create some resistance. So make sure this feels good and doesn't create any tension in your body. That goes for the rest of the prompts, too.

Meditate. How was it?

You may have never seen a meditation prompt in the beginning of a journal before, but the practice of focusing your mind on something neutral like white noise or a nonsensical mantra helps you in so many ways. It stops resistance, gets the flow of your bigger nonphysical energy going, and opens you up to a positive receiving mode. This practice is powerful and when you do it habitually, you will notice a vast improvement in your mood and how your days play out.

We've included a handy checklist so you can mark your progress and an area for you to note how it went. Maybe you tried a new sound to focus on and you loved it—you can mark that down to remember. Or perhaps you were distracted, that's OK—you can note that for the day if you'd like.

Positive Aspects: What do I value right now?

Now for something you're more familiar with: appreciating what's going well in your life. I like to include whatever comes to mind first. It's usually my cats and the trees I see out my window. Then I might get into memories that come up or the people in my life. No need to force things, just let whatever comes to mind that feels good roll onto the paper. It doesn't matter if it's the same every day, do your best to be present and not judge what you write down.

Daydreaming: What is getting ready for me?

Daydreaming is a practice of allowing yourself to relax enough so that you receive images of things that are swirling around in your vortex. What are you lining up with vibrationally? What are you getting ready to experience in your life? These are things that will show up in your daydreams. It's not necessary to see them in a visual way, it's ok to feel their essence or receive them like an idea.

Just write down what feels good, light, and exciting. If nothing comes to you, it's OK to skip this. Again, no need to force anything.

Intuitive Art Prompt: What do I want clarity on right now?

This drawing is telling me:

Intuitive Art is a process of asking your Higher Self questions and getting the answer in the form of color & scribbles. It's easy to learn and turns your intuition into a whole language instead of just those vague yes or no feelings in your body. You can take a free class to learn it at intuitiveartclass.com. It's worth the hour of your time and yields a lifetime of clarity!

This prompt and page gives you the opportunity to get clarity on any subject you want. The next page has an area for writing down the answer. This way, you can look back and reference the drawing and its wisdom again.

Inspired Actions for the Day:

This journal is meant to connect you with your Higher Self and to a place in your body that feels good. So when we include a place for action steps, it's meant for the ones that are inspired. Your Intuitive Art, daydreaming, or appreciation may have sparked an awareness of actions that would feel amazing today. That's what you want to write down here, not your entire daily to-do list. If you can prioritize this list, even better.

Epiphanies & Calibration:

Got more in you? Here's a place to keep writing. Go on a rampage of appreciation and list all of the amazing things in your life. Or, if you're feeling like a limiting belief has taken your attention, calibrate it to a place that feels better here.

Calibration just means meeting something where it is and moving it to where you want it to be. You do this slowly, bit by bit. With a soothing tone and never judgment, you can start in a negative place and move it up. Here's an example:

Say you're worried about going to the park for the day instead of working at your desk. A thought was activated in you that says, "I have so much to do, I won't be able to get everything done if I spend time driving to the park. My partner will think I don't take my work seriously, too. Maybe I shouldn't go." That's your baseline. You feel anxious and like it would be easier to just not go, even though the action was inspired. To calibrate it, just soothe yourself like this, "It's true that going to the park is unusual for me, but that doesn't mean I'm ditching my work. I can even tell my partner that I work better in the fresh air. They won't care anyway, I know that judgment is only in my head. I actually become more efficient when I'm in a beautiful environment. I think my assignment will benefit from me being there. And because I'll get it done faster, I can even take a walk. The drive time won't eat into my work time because I can receive ideas on the way there. Driving is always good for that!" Now you're up to speed with the idea and it feels good again, like it did when you received the inspiration. When you're calibrating, you will find the right words to use that feel true to you. It's possible on most subjects to move from negative to positive. But never force it. If it feels too difficult, change the subject and calibrate at a later time. Again, the point is to feel good!

My intentions for the month of:

You'll start off your month with a special page as well. This is designed to help you focus on what you want to feel, create, and experience. Focusing in this way adds momentum to your desires. It doesn't matter if these intentions play out in your daily experience. In your day to day, just practice aligning with feeling good.

Go be the deliberate creator of your life and enjoy this daily alignment journal.

<3 Rachel Archelaus, Founder of the Intuitive Art Academy

My intentions for the month of: _____

I want to feel:

_____
_____
_____
_____
_____
_____

I want to create:

_____
_____
_____
_____
_____
_____

I want to experience:

_____
_____
_____
_____
_____
_____

I will focus on the above to the best of my ability while also not ever making myself feel wrong. The point is to care for and nurture my relationship with myself so that things flow to me naturally. My higher self knows the pathway and by practicing the alignment process in this journal I will sync up with the bigger part of me to allow for effortless ease and abundance.

Date: _____

How do I want to feel today?
_____

Meditate. How was it?
_____

Positive Aspects: What do I value right now?
_____
_____
_____
_____
_____
_____
_____
_____
_____
_____

Daydream: What is getting ready for me?
_____
_____
_____
_____
_____
_____
_____
_____
_____
_____

Intuitive Art Prompt: What do I want clarity on right now?

This drawing is telling me:

_____
_____
_____
_____
_____
_____
_____
_____
_____

Inspired Actions for the Day:

○
○
○
○
○
○
○

Epiphanies & Calibration:

_____
_____
_____
_____
_____
_____
_____
_____
_____

Date: _____

How do I want to feel today?
_____

Meditate. How was it?
_____

Positive Aspects: What do I value right now?
_____
_____
_____
_____
_____
_____
_____
_____
_____

Daydream: What is getting ready for me?
_____
_____
_____
_____
_____
_____
_____
_____
_____

Intuitive Art Prompt: What do I want clarity on right now?

This drawing is telling me:

_____
_____
_____
_____
_____
_____
_____
_____
_____
_____

Inspired Actions for the Day:

-
-
-
-
-
-
-

Epiphanies & Calibration:

_____
_____
_____
_____
_____
_____
_____

Date: _____

How do I want to feel today?
_____

Meditate. How was it?
_____

Positive Aspects: What do I value right now?
_____
_____
_____
_____
_____
_____
_____
_____
_____

Daydream: What is getting ready for me?
_____
_____
_____
_____
_____
_____
_____
_____
_____

Intuitive Art Prompt: What do I want clarity on right now?

This drawing is telling me:
_____
_____
_____
_____
_____
_____
_____
_____
_____
_____

Inspired Actions for the Day:

○
○
○
○
○
○
○

Epiphanies & Calibration:
_____
_____
_____
_____
_____
_____
_____

Date: _____

How do I want to feel today?
_____

Meditate. How was it?
_____

Positive Aspects: What do I value right now?
_____
_____
_____
_____
_____
_____
_____
_____
_____
_____

Daydream: What is getting ready for me?
_____
_____
_____
_____
_____
_____
_____
_____
_____
_____

Intuitive Art Prompt: What do I want clarity on right now?

This drawing is telling me:

_____
_____
_____
_____
_____
_____
_____
_____
_____

Inspired Actions for the Day:

- ○
- ○
- ○
- ○
- ○
- ○
- ○

Epiphanies & Calibration:

_____
_____
_____
_____
_____
_____
_____
_____

Date: _____

How do I want to feel today?
_____

Meditate. How was it?
_____

Positive Aspects: What do I value right now?
_____
_____
_____
_____
_____
_____
_____
_____
_____

Daydream: What is getting ready for me?
_____
_____
_____
_____
_____
_____
_____
_____
_____

Intuitive Art Prompt: What do I want clarity on right now?

This drawing is telling me:

_____
_____
_____
_____
_____
_____
_____
_____
_____

Inspired Actions for the Day:

- ○
- ○
- ○
- ○
- ○
- ○
- ○

Epiphanies & Calibration:

_____
_____
_____
_____
_____
_____
_____
_____

Date: _____

How do I want to feel today?
_____

Meditate. How was it?
_____

Positive Aspects: What do I value right now?
_____
_____
_____
_____
_____
_____
_____
_____
_____

Daydream: What is getting ready for me?
_____
_____
_____
_____
_____
_____
_____
_____
_____

Intuitive Art Prompt: What do I want clarity on right now?

This drawing is telling me:

_____
_____
_____
_____
_____
_____
_____
_____
_____

Inspired Actions for the Day:

○
○
○
○
○
○
○

Epiphanies & Calibration:

_____
_____
_____
_____
_____
_____
_____
_____

Date: _____

How do I want to feel today?
_____

Meditate. How was it?
_____

Positive Aspects: What do I value right now?
_____
_____
_____
_____
_____
_____
_____
_____
_____
_____

Daydream: What is getting ready for me?
_____
_____
_____
_____
_____
_____
_____
_____
_____

Intuitive Art Prompt: What do I want clarity on right now?

This drawing is telling me:

_____
_____
_____
_____
_____
_____
_____
_____
_____

Inspired Actions for the Day:

○
○
○
○
○
○
○

Epiphanies & Calibration:

_____
_____
_____
_____
_____
_____
_____
_____

Date: _____

How do I want to feel today?
_____

Meditate. How was it?
_____

Positive Aspects: What do I value right now?
_____
_____
_____
_____
_____
_____
_____
_____
_____
_____

Daydream: What is getting ready for me?
_____
_____
_____
_____
_____
_____
_____
_____
_____
_____

Intuitive Art Prompt: What do I want clarity on right now?
___

This drawing is telling me:

_____
_____
_____
_____
_____
_____
_____
_____
_____

Inspired Actions for the Day:

- ○
- ○
- ○
- ○
- ○
- ○
- ○

Epiphanies & Calibration:

_____
_____
_____
_____
_____
_____
_____
_____

Date: _____

How do I want to feel today?
_____

Meditate. How was it?
_____

Positive Aspects: What do I value right now?
_____
_____
_____
_____
_____
_____
_____
_____
_____
_____

Daydream: What is getting ready for me?
_____
_____
_____
_____
_____
_____
_____
_____
_____
_____

Intuitive Art Prompt: What do I want clarity on right now?

This drawing is telling me:
___
___
___
___
___
___
___
___
___
___

Inspired Actions for the Day:

○
○
○
○
○
○
○

Epiphanies & Calibration:
___
___
___
___
___
___
___

Date: _____

How do I want to feel today?
_____

Meditate. How was it?
_____

Positive Aspects: What do I value right now?
_____
_____
_____
_____
_____
_____
_____
_____
_____

Daydream: What is getting ready for me?
_____
_____
_____
_____
_____
_____
_____
_____
_____
_____

Intuitive Art Prompt: What do I want clarity on right now?

This drawing is telling me:

_____
_____
_____
_____
_____
_____
_____
_____

Inspired Actions for the Day:

○
○
○
○
○
○
○

Epiphanies & Calibration:

_____
_____
_____
_____
_____
_____
_____
_____

Date: _____

How do I want to feel today?
_____

Meditate. How was it?
_____

Positive Aspects: What do I value right now?
_____
_____
_____
_____
_____
_____
_____
_____
_____
_____

Daydream: What is getting ready for me?
_____
_____
_____
_____
_____
_____
_____
_____
_____
_____

Intuitive Art Prompt: What do I want clarity on right now?

This drawing is telling me:
_____
_____
_____
_____
_____
_____
_____
_____
_____
_____

Inspired Actions for the Day:
- ○
- ○
- ○
- ○
- ○
- ○
- ○

Epiphanies & Calibration:
_____
_____
_____
_____
_____
_____
_____
_____

Date: _____

How do I want to feel today?
_____

Meditate. How was it?
_____

Positive Aspects: What do I value right now?
_____
_____
_____
_____
_____
_____
_____
_____
_____

Daydream: What is getting ready for me?
_____
_____
_____
_____
_____
_____
_____
_____
_____

Intuitive Art Prompt: What do I want clarity on right now?

This drawing is telling me:

_____
_____
_____
_____
_____
_____
_____
_____
_____

Inspired Actions for the Day:

○
○
○
○
○
○
○

Epiphanies & Calibration:

_____
_____
_____
_____
_____
_____
_____
_____

Date: _____

How do I want to feel today?
_____

Meditate. How was it?
_____

Positive Aspects: What do I value right now?
_____
_____
_____
_____
_____
_____
_____
_____
_____

Daydream: What is getting ready for me?
_____
_____
_____
_____
_____
_____
_____
_____
_____

Intuitive Art Prompt: What do I want clarity on right now?

This drawing is telling me:

_____
_____
_____
_____
_____
_____
_____
_____
_____
_____

Inspired Actions for the Day:

○
○
○
○
○
○
○

Epiphanies & Calibration:

_____
_____
_____
_____
_____
_____
_____
_____

Date: _____

How do I want to feel today?
_____

Meditate. How was it?
_____

Positive Aspects: What do I value right now?
_____
_____
_____
_____
_____
_____
_____
_____
_____
_____

Daydream: What is getting ready for me?
_____
_____
_____
_____
_____
_____
_____
_____
_____
_____

Intuitive Art Prompt: What do I want clarity on right now?

This drawing is telling me:
_____
_____
_____
_____
_____
_____
_____
_____
_____
_____

Inspired Actions for the Day:
- ○
- ○
- ○
- ○
- ○
- ○
- ○

Epiphanies & Calibration:
_____
_____
_____
_____
_____
_____
_____
_____

Date: _____

How do I want to feel today?
_____

Meditate. How was it?
_____

Positive Aspects: What do I value right now?
_____
_____
_____
_____
_____
_____
_____
_____
_____

Daydream: What is getting ready for me?
_____
_____
_____
_____
_____
_____
_____
_____
_____

Intuitive Art Prompt: What do I want clarity on right now?

This drawing is telling me:

_____
_____
_____
_____
_____
_____
_____
_____
_____

Inspired Actions for the Day:

○
○
○
○
○
○
○

Epiphanies & Calibration:

_____
_____
_____
_____
_____
_____
_____
_____
_____

Date: _____

How do I want to feel today?
_____

Meditate. How was it?
_____

Positive Aspects: What do I value right now?
_____
_____
_____
_____
_____
_____
_____
_____
_____
_____

Daydream: What is getting ready for me?
_____
_____
_____
_____
_____
_____
_____
_____
_____
_____

Intuitive Art Prompt: What do I want clarity on right now?

This drawing is telling me:

_____
_____
_____
_____
_____
_____
_____
_____
_____

Inspired Actions for the Day:

- ○
- ○
- ○
- ○
- ○
- ○
- ○

Epiphanies & Calibration:

_____
_____
_____
_____
_____
_____
_____
_____

Date: _____

How do I want to feel today?
_____

Meditate. How was it?
_____

Positive Aspects: What do I value right now?
_____
_____
_____
_____
_____
_____
_____
_____
_____
_____

Daydream: What is getting ready for me?
_____
_____
_____
_____
_____
_____
_____
_____
_____
_____

Intuitive Art Prompt: What do I want clarity on right now?

This drawing is telling me:

_____
_____
_____
_____
_____
_____
_____
_____
_____

Inspired Actions for the Day:

- ○
- ○
- ○
- ○
- ○
- ○
- ○

Epiphanies & Calibration:

_____
_____
_____
_____
_____
_____
_____
_____

Date: _____

How do I want to feel today?
_____

Meditate. How was it?
_____

Positive Aspects: What do I value right now?
_____
_____
_____
_____
_____
_____
_____
_____
_____

Daydream: What is getting ready for me?
_____
_____
_____
_____
_____
_____
_____
_____
_____

Intuitive Art Prompt: What do I want clarity on right now?

This drawing is telling me:

_____
_____
_____
_____
_____
_____
_____
_____
_____

Inspired Actions for the Day:

- ○
- ○
- ○
- ○
- ○
- ○
- ○

Epiphanies & Calibration:

_____
_____
_____
_____
_____
_____
_____

Date: _____

How do I want to feel today?
_____

Meditate. How was it?
_____

Positive Aspects: What do I value right now?
_____
_____
_____
_____
_____
_____
_____
_____
_____

Daydream: What is getting ready for me?
_____
_____
_____
_____
_____
_____
_____
_____
_____

Intuitive Art Prompt: What do I want clarity on right now?

This drawing is telling me:

_____
_____
_____
_____
_____
_____
_____
_____
_____

Inspired Actions for the Day:

○
○
○
○
○
○
○

Epiphanies & Calibration:

_____
_____
_____
_____
_____
_____
_____
_____

Date: _____

How do I want to feel today?
_____

Meditate. How was it?
_____

Positive Aspects: What do I value right now?
_____
_____
_____
_____
_____
_____
_____
_____
_____

Daydream: What is getting ready for me?
_____
_____
_____
_____
_____
_____
_____
_____
_____

Intuitive Art Prompt: What do I want clarity on right now?

This drawing is telling me:

_____
_____
_____
_____
_____
_____
_____
_____
_____

Inspired Actions for the Day:

○
○
○
○
○
○
○

Epiphanies & Calibration:

_____
_____
_____
_____
_____
_____
_____
_____

Date: _____

How do I want to feel today?
_____

Meditate. How was it?
_____

Positive Aspects: What do I value right now?
_____
_____
_____
_____
_____
_____
_____
_____
_____
_____

Daydream: What is getting ready for me?
_____
_____
_____
_____
_____
_____
_____
_____
_____
_____

Intuitive Art Prompt: What do I want clarity on right now?

This drawing is telling me:

_____
_____
_____
_____
_____
_____
_____
_____
_____

Inspired Actions for the Day:

○
○
○
○
○
○
○

Epiphanies & Calibration:

_____
_____
_____
_____
_____
_____
_____
_____

Date: _____

How do I want to feel today?
_____

Meditate. How was it?
_____

Positive Aspects: What do I value right now?
_____
_____
_____
_____
_____
_____
_____
_____
_____

Daydream: What is getting ready for me?
_____
_____
_____
_____
_____
_____
_____
_____
_____

Intuitive Art Prompt: What do I want clarity on right now?

This drawing is telling me:

_____
_____
_____
_____
_____
_____
_____
_____
_____

Inspired Actions for the Day:

○
○
○
○
○
○
○

Epiphanies & Calibration:

_____
_____
_____
_____
_____
_____
_____
_____

Date: _____

How do I want to feel today?
_____

Meditate. How was it?
_____

Positive Aspects: What do I value right now?
_____
_____
_____
_____
_____
_____
_____
_____
_____

Daydream: What is getting ready for me?
_____
_____
_____
_____
_____
_____
_____
_____
_____
_____

Intuitive Art Prompt: What do I want clarity on right now?

This drawing is telling me:

_____
_____
_____
_____
_____
_____
_____
_____
_____

Inspired Actions for the Day:

○
○
○
○
○
○
○

Epiphanies & Calibration:

_____
_____
_____
_____
_____
_____
_____

Date: _____

How do I want to feel today?
_____

Meditate. How was it?
_____

Positive Aspects: What do I value right now?
_____
_____
_____
_____
_____
_____
_____
_____
_____

Daydream: What is getting ready for me?
_____
_____
_____
_____
_____
_____
_____
_____
_____
_____

Intuitive Art Prompt: What do I want clarity on right now?

This drawing is telling me:

_____
_____
_____
_____
_____
_____
_____
_____
_____
_____

Inspired Actions for the Day:

- ○
- ○
- ○
- ○
- ○
- ○
- ○

Epiphanies & Calibration:

_____
_____
_____
_____
_____
_____
_____
_____

Date: _____

How do I want to feel today?
_____

Meditate. How was it?
_____

Positive Aspects: What do I value right now?
_____
_____
_____
_____
_____
_____
_____
_____
_____
_____

Daydream: What is getting ready for me?
_____
_____
_____
_____
_____
_____
_____
_____
_____
_____

Intuitive Art Prompt: What do I want clarity on right now?

This drawing is telling me:

_____
_____
_____
_____
_____
_____
_____
_____
_____

Inspired Actions for the Day:

○
○
○
○
○
○
○

Epiphanies & Calibration:

_____
_____
_____
_____
_____
_____
_____
_____

Date: _____

How do I want to feel today?
_____

Meditate. How was it?
_____

Positive Aspects: What do I value right now?
_____
_____
_____
_____
_____
_____
_____
_____
_____
_____

Daydream: What is getting ready for me?
_____
_____
_____
_____
_____
_____
_____
_____
_____
_____

Intuitive Art Prompt: What do I want clarity on right now?

This drawing is telling me:

_____
_____
_____
_____
_____
_____
_____
_____
_____

Inspired Actions for the Day:

○
○
○
○
○
○
○

Epiphanies & Calibration:

_____
_____
_____
_____
_____
_____
_____
_____

Date: _____

How do I want to feel today?
_____

Meditate. How was it?
_____

Positive Aspects: What do I value right now?
_____
_____
_____
_____
_____
_____
_____
_____
_____

Daydream: What is getting ready for me?
_____
_____
_____
_____
_____
_____
_____
_____
_____

Intuitive Art Prompt: What do I want clarity on right now?

This drawing is telling me:

_____
_____
_____
_____
_____
_____
_____
_____
_____

Inspired Actions for the Day:

- ○
- ○
- ○
- ○
- ○
- ○
- ○

Epiphanies & Calibration:

_____
_____
_____
_____
_____
_____
_____
_____
_____

Date: _____

How do I want to feel today?
_____

Meditate. How was it?
_____

Positive Aspects: What do I value right now?
_____
_____
_____
_____
_____
_____
_____
_____
_____

Daydream: What is getting ready for me?
_____
_____
_____
_____
_____
_____
_____
_____
_____

Intuitive Art Prompt: What do I want clarity on right now?

This drawing is telling me:

_____
_____
_____
_____
_____
_____
_____
_____
_____
_____

Inspired Actions for the Day:

- ○
- ○
- ○
- ○
- ○
- ○
- ○

Epiphanies & Calibration:

_____
_____
_____
_____
_____
_____
_____
_____

Date: _____

How do I want to feel today?
_____

Meditate. How was it?
_____

Positive Aspects: What do I value right now?
_____
_____
_____
_____
_____
_____
_____
_____
_____
_____

Daydream: What is getting ready for me?
_____
_____
_____
_____
_____
_____
_____
_____
_____
_____

Intuitive Art Prompt: What do I want clarity on right now?
_____

This drawing is telling me:

_____
_____
_____
_____
_____
_____
_____
_____
_____
_____

Inspired Actions for the Day:

- ○
- ○
- ○
- ○
- ○
- ○
- ○

Epiphanies & Calibration:

_____
_____
_____
_____
_____
_____
_____

Date: _____

How do I want to feel today?
_____

Meditate. How was it?
_____

Positive Aspects: What do I value right now?
_____
_____
_____
_____
_____
_____
_____
_____
_____

Daydream: What is getting ready for me?
_____
_____
_____
_____
_____
_____
_____
_____
_____

Intuitive Art Prompt: What do I want clarity on right now?

This drawing is telling me:

_____
_____
_____
_____
_____
_____
_____
_____
_____
_____

Inspired Actions for the Day:

- ◯
- ◯
- ◯
- ◯
- ◯
- ◯
- ◯

Epiphanies & Calibration:

_____
_____
_____
_____
_____
_____
_____

Date: _____

How do I want to feel today?
_____

Meditate. How was it?
_____

Positive Aspects: What do I value right now?
_____
_____
_____
_____
_____
_____
_____
_____
_____
_____

Daydream: What is getting ready for me?
_____
_____
_____
_____
_____
_____
_____
_____
_____
_____

Intuitive Art Prompt: What do I want clarity on right now?

This drawing is telling me:

_____
_____
_____
_____
_____
_____
_____
_____
_____

Inspired Actions for the Day:

○
○
○
○
○
○
○

Epiphanies & Calibration:

_____
_____
_____
_____
_____
_____
_____
_____